Anonymous

Treason and Rebellion

Being in Part the Legislation of Congress and of the State of California

Anonymous

Treason and Rebellion
Being in Part the Legislation of Congress and of the State of California

ISBN/EAN: 9783744711869

Printed in Europe, USA, Canada, Australia, Japan

Cover: Foto ©Suzi / pixelio.de

More available books at **www.hansebooks.com**

TREASON AND REBELLION:

BEING IN PART THE

LEGISLATION OF CONGRESS

AND OF

THE STATE OF CALIFORNIA

THEREON, TOGETHER WITH THE RECENT

CHARGE BY JUDGE FIELD,

OF THE U. S. SUPREME COURT,

DELIVERED TO THE GRAND JURY IN ATTENDANCE AT THE JUNE TERM, EIGHTEEN
HUNDRED AND SIXTY-THREE, OF THE U. S. CIRCUIT COURT FOR
THE NORTHERN DISTRICT OF CALIFORNIA.

WITH NOTES.

———————

SAN FRANCISCO:

PRINTED BY TOWNE & BACON, BOOK AND JOB PRINTERS,

No. 536 Clay Street, opposite Leidesdorff.

1863.

LEGISLATION ON TREASON AND REBELLION.

THE existing rebellion against the United States has given rise to much legislation concerning treason and kindred offenses of a lesser grade. The various Acts of Congress are scattered through the statutes at large for 1861-2-3, and these having been received in this State but recently, and only in limited numbers, there is a lack of information on the subject among the general public, and even in the legal profession, which it is the object of the present publication partially to supply. The majority of readers will probably be surprised to see the thoroughness of Congressional action upon the subject, and the obstacles which have been thrown in the way of every grade of disloyalty.

An act passed July 31st, 1861, declares it to be a high crime, punishable by fine, or imprisonment for a term of years, or both, for two or more persons to conspire to forcibly destroy, or levy war against, or oppose the authority of the United States Government; or to forcibly prevent or hinder the execution of any law of the United States, or to prevent, by force or threat, any person from holding office under the United States.

An act of August 6th, 1861, makes it a high misdemeanor, punishable by fine and imprisonment for any person to recruit soldiers or sailors to engage in armed hostility to the Government, or to enlist in such service.

By another enactment, approved the same day, all property, sold or given, to be used in aiding combinations against the Government which may have been declared by proclamation of the President too powerful to be suppressed by the ordinary course of judicial proceedings, is declared lawful subject of prize, capture, and confiscation.

The act of July 17th, 1862, " to suppress Insurrection, to punish Treason and Rebellion, to seize and confiscate the Property of Rebels, and for other purposes," prescribes the penalty for treason, and also for the crime of inciting, assisting, or engaging in any rebellion or insurrection against the authority or laws of the United States; and makes it the duty of the President to cause the seizure of all the property and effects of persons engaged in the Southern Rebellion, or aiding or abetting the same, and to apply the proceeds of such seizures for the support of the National armies.

By an act approved February 25th, 1863, correspondence with rebels for the purpose of defeating or weakening Government measures, is declared to be a high misdemeanor to be punished by fine and imprisonment.

An act approved March 12th, 1863, provides for the confiscation of all property brought from rebellious States into other States, by any person other than a Government agent, unless under a lawful clearance by the proper officer of the Treasury Department, and declares the person so offending to be guilty of a misdemeanor punishable by fine or imprisonment.

By various enactments the most searching oaths of allegiance are required to be taken by all persons in the civil, military, or naval service of the United States; all officers, clerks, and employés of Departments, all who are in any manner connected with the mail service; all cadets at West Point; all commanders of American vessels sailing for foreign ports; all persons presenting claims for settlement at the departments or bureaus at Washington, and, on motion of the United States Attorney, or in the discretion of the Court, by all grand and petit jurors in the United States Courts.

By the act of June 17th, 1862, various disloyal practices, therein named, disqualify persons guilty thereof from serving as grand or petit jurors in the United States Courts.

In these pages will be found in full the Acts of Congress referred to.

The Legislature of the State of California, at the session of 1863, passed several acts prescribing penalties for offenses against the General Government. The displaying of a rebel flag, or of the flag of any public enemy of the United States is made punishable by fine or imprisonment, or both. Fitting out vessels as privateers against the property of citizens of the United States, or aiding to do so; setting on foot any military expedition against United States authority, or aiding to do so, and accepting any commission, or letter of marque from the authorities of the so-called Confederate States, are declared felonies punishable by death or imprisonment, at the discretion of the jury. Attorneys in the State Courts are required to take an oath of allegiance to the United States; and the plaintiff in a civil action, if declared by the defendant to be disloyal, is required to take the same oath, in order to maintain his standing in Court. Persons making locations on the public lands, of the State are also required to take an oath of like character. Another act declares all public expressions of sympathy with the rebel cause to be misdemeanors punishable by fine or imprisonment, or both. These acts are herein given entire.

To the Federal and State enactments concerning treason and rebellion, is added the recent charge of Judge Field to the Grand Jury of the United States Circuit Court for the Northern District of California, together with citations from several opinions and authorities upon the subject under consideration. While the charge gives a brief and general statement of the law of treason, it does not purport to give a full exposition. Such exposition is found in the treatises of Foster, Hale, Hawkins, and East, in various decisions of the U. S. Supreme Court, and in opinions and charges of the Judges, from which citations are made. The debate in the Senate of the United States on the second section of the act of July 17th, 1862, is also given, as throwing light upon a class of offenses which are not therein designated as treason, and are not considered in the charge of Judge Field.

CHAP. XXXIII.—*An Act to define and punish certain Conspiracies.*—Approved July 31st, 1861.

Be it enacted by the Senate and House of Representatives of the United States of America in Congress assembled, That if two or more persons within any State or Territory of the United States shall conspire together to overthrow, or to put down, or to destroy by force, the Government of the United States, or to levy war against the United States, or to oppose by force the authority of the Government of the United States ; or by force to prevent, hinder, or delay the execution of any law of the United States ; or by force to seize, take, or possess any property of the United States against the will or contrary to the authority of the United States ; or by force, or intimidation, or threat to prevent any person from accepting or holding any office, or trust, or place of confidence, under the United States ; each and every person so offending shall be guilty of a high crime, and upon conviction thereof in any District or Circuit Court of the United States, having jurisdiction thereof, or District or Supreme Court of any Territory of the United States having jurisdiction thereof, shall be punished by a fine not less than five hundred dollars and not more than five thousand dollars ; or by imprisonment, with or without hard labor, as the Court shall determine, for a period not less than six months nor greater than six years, or by both such fine and imprisonment.

CHAP. LVI.—*An Act to punish certain Crimes against the United States.*—Approved August 6th, 1861.

Be it enacted by the Senate and House of Representatives of the United States of America in Congress assembled, That if any person shall be guilty of the act of recruiting soldiers or sailors in any State or Territory of the United States to engage in armed hostility against the United States, or who shall open a recruiting station for the enlistment of such persons, either as regulars or volunteers, to serve as aforesaid, shall be guilty of a high misdemeanor, and upon conviction in any Court of Record having jurisdiction of the offense, shall be fined a sum not less than two hundred dollars nor more than one thousand dollars; and confined and imprisoned for a period not less than one year nor more than five years.

SEC. 2. *And be it further enacted,* That the person so enlisted, or engaged as regular or volunteer, shall be fined in a like manner a sum of one hundred dollars, and imprisoned not less than one nor more than three years.

CHAP. LX.—*An Act to confiscate Property used for Insurrectionary Purposes.*—Approved August 6th, 1861.

Be it enacted by the Senate and House of Representatives of the United States of America in Congress assembled, That if, during the present or any future insurrection against the Government of the United States, after the President of the United States shall have declared, by proclamation, that the laws of the United States are opposed, and the execution thereof obstructed, by combinations too powerful to be suppressed by the ordinary course of judicial proceedings, or by the power vested in the Marshals by law, any person or persons, his, her, or their agent, attorney, or employé, shall purchase or acquire, sell or give, any property of whatsoever kind or description with intent to use or employ the same, or suffer the same to be used or employed, in aiding, abetting, or promoting such insurrection or resistance to the laws, or any person or persons engaged therein ; or if any person or persons, being the owner or owners of any such property, shall knowingly use or employ, or consent to the use or employment of the same as aforesaid, all such property is hereby declared to be lawful subject of prize and capture wherever found ; and it shall be the duty of the President of the United States to cause the same to be seized, confiscated, and condemned.

SEC. 2. *And be it further enacted,* That such prizes and capture shall be condemned in the District or Circuit Court of the United States having jurisdiction of the amount, or in admiralty in any District in which the same may be seized, or into which they may be taken and proceedings first instituted.

SEC. 3. *And be it further enacted,* That the Attorney-General, or any District Attorney of the United States in which said property may at the time be, may institute the proceedings of condemnation, and in such case they shall be wholly for the benefit of the United States ; or any person may file an information with such Attorney, in which case the proceedings shall be for the use of such informer and the United States in equal parts.

SEC. 4. *And be it further enacted,* That whenever hereafter, during the present insurrection against the Government of the United States, any person claimed to be held to labor or service under the law of any State, shall be required or permitted by the person to whom such labor or service is claimed to be due, or by the lawful agent of such person, to take up arms against the United States, or shall be required or permitted by the person to whom such labor or service is claimed to be due, or his lawful agent, to work or to be employed in or upon any fort, navy yard, dock, armory, ship, entrenchment, or in any military or naval service whatsoever, against the Government and lawful authority of the United States, then, and in every such case, the person to whom such labor or service is claimed to be due shall forfeit his claim to such labor, any law of the State or of the United States to the contrary notwithstanding. And whenever thereafter the person claiming such labor or service shall seek to enforce his claim, it shall be a full and sufficient answer to such claim that the person whose service or labor is claimed had been employed in hostile service against the Government of the United States, contrary to the provisions of this act.

CHAP. CIII.—*An Act defining additional causes of Challenge and prescribing an additional Oath for Grand and Petit Jurors in the United States Courts.*— Approved June 17th, 1862.

Be it enacted by the Senate and House of Representatives of the United States of America in Congress assembled, That, in addition to the existing causes of disqualification and challenge of grand and petit jurors in the Courts of the United States, the following are hereby declared and established, namely : without duress and coercion to have taken up arms, or to have joined any insurrection and rebellion, against the United States ; to have adhered to any rebellion, giving it aid or comfort ; to have given, directly or indirectly, any assistance in money, arms, horses, clothes, or any thing whatever, to or for the use or benefit of any person or persons whom the person giving such assistance knew to have joined, or to be about to join, any insurrection or rebellion, or to have resisted, or to be about to resist with force of arms, the execution of the laws of the United States, or whom he had good ground to believe had joined, or was about to join, any insurrection or rebellion, or had resisted, or was about to resist, with force of arms, the execution of the laws of the United States, and to have counseled and advised any person or persons to join any insurrection and rebellion, or. to resist with force of arms the laws of the United States.

SEC. 2. *And be it further enacted,* That at each and every term of any Court of the United States, the District Attorney, or other person acting for and on behalf of the United States in said Court, may move, and the Court in their discretion may require the Clerk to tender to each and every person who may be summoned to serve as a grand or petit juror or venireman or talesman in said Court, the following oath or affirmation, viz. : " You do solemnly swear (or affirm, as the case may be) that you will support the Constitution of the United States of America ; that you have not, without duress and constraint, taken up arms, or joined any insurrection or rebellion against the United States ; that you have not adhered to any insurrection or rebellion, giving it aid and comfort ; that you have not, directly or indirectly, given any assistance in money, or any other thing, to any person or persons whom you knew, or had good ground to believe, had joined or was about to join, said insurrection and rebellion, or had resisted, or was about to resist, with force of arms, the execution of the laws of the United States ; and that you have not counseled or advised any person or persons to join any rebellion against, or to resist with force of arms, the laws of the United States." Any person or persons declining to take said oath shall be discharged by the Court from serving on the grand or petit jury, or venire, to which he may have been summoned.

SEC. 3. *And be it further enacted,* That each and every person who shall take the oath herein prescribed, and who shall swear falsely to any matter of fact embraced by it, shall be held to have committed the crime of perjury, and shall be subject to the pains and penalties declared against that crime.

CHAP. CXXVIII.—*An Act to prescribe an Oath of Office, and for other Purposes.*— Approved July 2d, 1862.

Be it enacted by the Senate and House of Representatives of the United States of America in Congress assembled, That hereafter every person elected or appointed to any office of honor or profit under the Government of the United States, either in the civil, military, or naval departments of the public service, excepting the President of the United States, shall, before entering upon the duties of such office, and before being entitled to any of the salary or other emoluments thereof, take and subscribe the following oath or affirmation : " I, A. B., do solemnly swear (or affirm) that I have never voluntarily borne arms against the United States since I have been a citizen thereof; that I have voluntarily given no aid, countenance, counsel, or encouragement to persons engaged in armed hostility thereto ; that I have neither sought nor accepted, nor attempted to exercise, the functions of any office whatever, under any authority or pretended authority in hostility to the United States ; that I have not yielded a voluntary support to any pretended government, authority, power or constitution within the United States, hostile or inimical thereto.   And I do further swear (or affirm) that, to the best of my knowledge and ability, I will support and defend the Constitution of the United States, against all enemies, foreign and domestic ; that I will bear true faith and allegiance to the same ; that I take this obligation freely, without any mental reservation or purpose of evasion, and that I will well and faithfully discharge the duties of the office on which I am about to enter, so help me God ;" which said oath, so taken and signed, shall be preserved among the files of the Court, House of Congress, or Department to which the said office may appertain.   And any person who shall falsely take the said oath shall be guilty of perjury, and on conviction, in addition to the penalties now prescribed for that offense, shall be deprived of his office and rendered incapable forever after of holding any office or place under the United States.

CHAP. CXCV.—*An Act to suppress Insurrection, to punish Treason and Rebellion, to seize and confiscate the Property of Rebels, and for other Purposes.*—Approved July 17th, 1862.

Be it enacted by the Senate and House of Representatives of the United States of America in Congress assembled, That every person who shall hereafter commit the crime of treason against the United States, and shall be adjudged guilty thereof, shall suffer death, and all his slaves, if any, shall be declared and made free ; or, at the discretion of the Court, he shall be imprisoned for not less than five years and fined not less than ten thousand dollars, and all his slaves, if any, shall be declared and made free ; said fine shall be levied and collected on any or all of the property, real and personal, excluding slaves, of which the said person so convicted was the owner at the time of committing the said crime, any sale or conveyance to the contrary notwithstanding.

SEC. 2. *And be it further enacted,* That if any person shall hereafter incite, set on foot, assist, or engage in any rebellion or insurrection against the authority of the United States, or the laws thereof, or shall give aid or comfort thereto, or shall engage in or give aid and comfort to any such existing rebellion or insurrection, and be convicted thereof, such person shall be punished by imprisonment for a period not exceeding ten years, or by a fine not exceeding ten thousand dollars, and by the liberation of all his slaves, if any he have ; or by both said punishments, at the discretion of the Court.

SEC. 3. *And be it further enacted,* That every person guilty of either of the offenses described in this act shall be forever incapable and disqualified to hold any office under the United States.

SEC. 4. *And be it further enacted,* That this act shall not be construed in any way to affect or alter the prosecution, conviction, or punishment of any person or persons guilty of treason against the United States before the passage of this act, unless such person is convicted under this act.

SEC. 5. *And be it further enacted*, That, to insure the speedy termination of the present rebellion, it shall be the duty of the President of the United States to cause the seizure of all the estate and property, money, stocks, credits, and effects of the persons hereinafter named in this section, and to apply and use the same and the proceeds thereof for the support of the army of the United States, that is to say :

First. Of any person hereafter acting as an officer of the army or navy of the rebels in arms against the Government of the United States.

Secondly. Of any person hereafter acting as President, Vice President, Member of Congress, Judge of any Court, Cabinet officer, Foreign Minister, Commissioner, or Consul of the so-called Confederate States of America.

Thirdly. Of any person acting as Governor of a State, Member of a Convention or Legislature, or Judge of any Court of any of the so-called Confederate States of America.

Fourthly. Of any person who, having held an office of honor, trust, or profit in the United States, shall hereafter hold an office in the so-called Confederate States of America.

Fifthly. Of any person hereafter holding any office or agency under the government of the so-called Confederate States of America, or under any of the several States of the said Confederacy, or the laws thereof, whether such office or agency be national, State, or municipal in its name or character : *Provided,* That the persons, thirdly, fourthly, and fifthly, above described, shall have accepted their appointment or election since the date of the pretended ordinance of secession of the State, or shall have taken an oath of allegiance to, or to support the Constitution of the so-called Confederate States.

Sixthly. Of any person who, owning property in any loyal State or Territory of the United States, or in the District of Columbia, shall hereafter assist and give aid and comfort to such rebellion ; and all sales, transfers, or conveyances of any such property shall be null and void ; and it shall be a sufficient bar to any suit brought by such person for the possession or the use of such property, or any of it, to allege and prove that he is one of the persons described in this section.

SEC. 6. *And be it further enacted*, That if any person within any State or Territory of the United States, other than those named as aforesaid, after the passage of this act, being engaged in armed rebellion against the Government of the United States, or aiding or abetting such rebellion, shall not, within sixty days after public warning and proclamation duly given and made by the President of the United States, cease to aid, countenance, and abet such rebellion, and return to his allegiance to the United States, all the estate and property, moneys, stocks, and credits of such person shall be liable to seizure as aforesaid, and it shall be the duty of the President to seize and use them as aforesaid or the proceeds thereof. And all sales, transfers, or conveyances, of any such property after the expiration of the said sixty days from the date of such warning and proclamation shall be null and void ; and it shall be a sufficient bar to any suit brought by such person for the possession or the use of such property, or any of it, to allege and prove that he is one of the persons described in this section.*

---

* The proclamation of the President here designated was made on the twenty-fifth of July, 1862. (See Appendix to twelfth volume of Statutes at Large, p. 1266.)

SEC. 7. *And be it further enacted*, That to secure the condemnation and sale of any of such property, after the same shall have been seized, so that it may be made available for the purpose aforesaid, proceedings *in rem* shall be instituted in the name of the United States in any District Court thereof, or in any Territorial Court, or in the United States District Court for the District of Columbia, within which the property above described, or any part thereof, may be found, or into which the same, if movable, may first be brought, which proceedings shall conform 'as nearly as may be to proceedings in admiralty or revenue cases, and if said property, whether real or personal, shall be found to have belonged to a person engaged in rebellion, or who has given aid or comfort thereto, the same shall be condemned as enemies' property and become the property of the United States, and may be disposed of as the Court shall decree, and the proceeds thereof paid into the treasury of the United States for the purposes aforesaid.

SEC. 8. *And be it further enacted*, That the several Courts aforesaid shall have power to make such orders, establish such forms of decree and sale, and direct such deeds and conveyances to be executed and delivered by the Marshals thereof where real estate shall be the subject of sale, as shall fitly and efficiently effect, the purposes of this act, and vest in the purchasers of such property good and valid titles thereto. And the said Courts shall have power to allow such fees and charges of their officers as shall be reasonable and proper in the premises.

SEC. 9. *And be it further enacted*, That all slaves of persons who shall hereafter be engaged in rebellion against the Government of the United States, or who shall in any way give aid or comfort thereto, escaping from such persons and taking refuge within the lines of the army ; and all slaves captured from such persons or deserted by them and coming under the control of the Government of the United States ; and all slaves of such persons found on [or] being within any place occupied by rebel forces and afterwards occupied by the forces of the United States, shall be deemed captives of war, and shall be forever free of their servitude, and not again held as slaves.

SEC. 10. *And be it further enacted*, That no slave escaping into any State, Territory, or the District of Columbia, from any other State, shall be delivered up, or in any way impeded or hindered of his liberty, except for crime or some offense against the laws, unless the person claiming said fugitive shall first make oath that the person to whom the labor or service of such fugitive is alleged to be due is his lawful owner, and has not borne arms against the United States in the present rebellion, nor in any way given aid or comfort thereto ; and no person engaged in the military or naval service of the United States shall, under any pretense whatever, assume to decide on the validity of the claim of any person to the service or labor of any other person, or surrender up any such person to the claimant, on pain of being dismissed from the service.

SEC. 11. *And be it further enacted*, That the President of the United States is authorized to employ as many persons of African descent as he may deem necessary and proper for the suppression of this rebellion, and for this purpose he may organize and use them in such manner as he may judge best for the public welfare.

SEC. 12. *And be it further enacted*, That the President of the United States is hereby authorized to make provision for the transportation, colonization, and settlement, in some tropical country beyond the limits of the United States, of such persons of the African race, made free by the provisions of this act, as may be willing to emigrate, having first obtained the consent of the government of said country to their protection and settlement within the same, with all the rights and privileges of freemen.

Sec. 13. *And be it further enacted,* That the President is hereby authorized, at any time hereafter, by proclamation, to extend to persons who may have participated in the existing rebellion in any State or part thereof, pardon and amnesty, with such exceptions and at such time and on such conditions as he may deem expedient for the public welfare.

Sec. 14. *And be it further enacted,* That the Courts of the United States shall have full power to institute proceedings, make orders and decrees, issue process, and do all other things necessary to carry this act into effect.*

Chap. LX.—*An Act to Prevent Correspondence with Rebels.*—Approved February 25, 1863.

Be it enacted by the Senate and House of Representatives of the United States of America in Congress assembled, That if any person, being a resident of the United States, or being a citizen thereof, and residing in any foreign country, shall, without the permission or authority of the Government of the United States, and with the intent to defeat the measures of the said Government, or to weaken in any way their efficacy, hold or commence, directly or indirectly, any correspondence or intercourse, written or verbal, with the present pretended rebel Government, or with any officer or agent thereof, or with any other individual acting or sympathizing therewith; or if any such person above mentioned, not duly authorized, shall counsel or assist in any such correspondence or intercourse, with intent as aforesaid, he shall be deemed guilty of a high misdemeanor, and, on conviction before any Court of the United States, having jurisdiction thereof, shall be punished by a fine not exceeding ten thousand dollars, and by imprisonment not less than six months nor exceeding five years.

Sec. 2. *And be it further enacted,* That where the offense is committed in any foreign country, the District Court of the United States for the district where the offender shall be first arrested shall have jurisdiction thereof.

Chap. CXX.—*An Act to provide for the collection of abandoned Property and for the prevention of Frauds in Insurrectionary Districts of the United States.*—Approved March 3, 1863.

Be it enacted by the Senate and House of Representatives of the United States of America in Congress assembled, That it shall be lawful for the Secretary of the

---

* On the same day, July 17th, 1862, the following joint resolution explanatory of this act was passed:

Resolved by the Senate and House of Representatives of the United States of America in Congress assembled, That the provisions of the third clause of the fifth section of "An Act to suppress insurrection, to punish treason and rebellion, to seize and confiscate the property of rebels, and for other purposes," shall be so construed as not to apply to any act or acts done prior to the passage thereof; nor to include any member of a State Legislature, or Judge of any State Court, who has not in accepting or entering upon his office, taken an oath to support the constitution of the so-called "Confederate States of America;" nor shall any punishment or proceedings under said act be so construed as to work a forfeiture of the real estate of the offender beyond his natural life.

Treasury, from and after the passage of this Act, as he shall from time to time see fit, to appoint a special agent or agents to receive and collect all abandoned or captured property in any State or Territory, or any portion of any State or Territory, of the United States, designated as in insurrection against the lawful Government of the United States by the proclamation of the President of July first, eighteen hundred and sixty-two : *Provided*, That such property shall not include any kind or description which has been used, or which was intended to be used, for waging or carrying on war against the United States, such as arms, ordnance, ships, steamboats, or other water craft, and the furniture, forage, military supplies, or munitions of war.

SEC. 2. *And be it further enacted*, That any part of the goods or property received or collected by such agent or agents may be appropriated to public use on due appraisement and certificate thereof, or forwarded to any place of sale within the loyal states, as the public interests may require ; and all sales of such property shall be at auction to the highest bidder, and the proceeds thereof shall be paid into the treasury of the United States.

SEC. 3. *And be it further enacted*, That the Secretary of the Treasury may require the special agents appointed under this Act to give a bond, with such securities and in such amount as he shall deem necessary, and to require the increase of said amounts, and the strengthening of said security, as circumstances may demand ; and he shall also cause a book or books of account to be kept, showing from whom such property was received, the cost of transportation, and proceeds of the sale thereof. And any person claiming to have been the owner of any such abandoned or captured property may, at any time within two years after the suppression of the rebellion, prefer his claim to the proceeds thereof in the Court of Claims ; and on proof to the satisfaction of said court of his ownership of said property, of his right to the proceeds thereof, and that he has never given any aid or comfort to the present rebellion, to receive the residue of such proceeds, after the deduction of any purchase-money which may have been paid, together with the expense of transportation and sale of said property, and any other lawful expenses attending the disposition thereof.

SEC. 4. *And be it further enacted*, That all property coming into any of the United States not declared in insurrection as aforesaid, from within any of the States declared in insurrection, through or by any other person than any agent duly appointed under the provisions of this Act, or under a lawful clearance by the proper officer of the Treasury Department, shall be confiscated to the use of the Government of the United States. And the proceedings for the condemnation and sale of any such property shall be instituted and conducted under the direction of the Secretary of the Treasury, in the mode prescribed by the eighty-ninth and ninetieth sections of the Act of March second, seventeen hundred and ninety-nine, entitled "An Act to regulate the collection of duties on imports and tonnage." And any agent or agents, person or persons, by or through whom such property shall come within the lines of the United States unlawfully, as aforesaid, shall be judged guilty of a misdemeanor, and on conviction thereof shall be fined in any sum not exceeding one thousand dollars, or imprisoned for any time not exceeding one year, or both, at the discretion of the court. And the fines, penalties, and forfeitures accruing under this Act may be mitigated or remitted in the mode prescribed by the Act of March three, seventeen hundred and ninety-seven, or in such manner, in special cases, as the Secretary of the Treasury may prescribe.

SEC. 5. *And be it further enacted*, That the fifth section of the "Act to further provide for the collection of the revenue upon the northern, north-eastern, and north-western frontier, and for other purposes," approved July fourteen, eighteen hundred and sixty-two, shall be so construed as to allow the temporary officers which have been or may be appointed at ports which have been or may be opened or established in States declared to be in insurrection by the proclamation of the President on the first of July, eighteen hundred and sixty-two, the same compensation which by law is allowed to permanent officers of the same position, or the ordinary compensation of special agents, as the Secretary of the Treasury may determine.

SEC. 6. *And be it further enacted*, That it shall be the duty of every officer or private of the regular or volunteer forces of the United States, or any officer, sailor, or marine in the naval service of the United States upon the inland waters of the United States, who may take or receive any such abandoned property, or cotton, sugar, rice, or tabacco, from persons in such insurrectionary districts, or have it under his control, to turn the same over to an agent appointed as aforesaid, who shall give a receipt therefor; and in case he shall refuse or neglect so to do, he shall be tried by a court-martial, and shall be dismissed from the service, or, if an officer, reduced to the ranks, or suffer such other punishment as said court shall order, with the approval of the President of the United States.

SEC. 7. *And be it further enacted*, That none of the provisions of this Act shall apply to any lawful maritime prize by the naval forces of the United States.

ACTS OF THE LEGISLATURE OF CALIFORNIA.

CHAP. CCLXIV.—*An Act supplementary to an Act entitled an Act concerning Crimes and Punishments, passed April sixteenth, one thousand eight hundred and fifty.—* Approved April 20, 1863.

The People of the State of California,
represented in Senate and Assembly, do enact as follows:

SECTION 1. Every person who shall expose to public view, on his own premises or elsewhere, or suffer to be exposed to public view on his own premises, any flag, or device, of the description used, or reputed to be used, by any rebels against the authority of this State, or of the United States, or by any public enemies of this State, or of the United States, shall be deemed guilty of a misdemeanor, and shall be punished by a fine not exceeding three hundred dollars, or by imprisonment in the County Jail for a term not exceeding sixty days, or by such fine and imprisonment both, at the discretion of the Court having cognizance of the offense.

SEC. 2. Such flag or device so exhibited, with the apparatus connected therewith, shall be deemed a nuisance, and any Constable of the township in which the same shall be so exhibited, or the Sheriff, or a Deputy Sheriff, or any other peace officer of the county in which the same shall be so exhibited, taking sufficient assistance therefor, may seize and destroy the same.

SEC. 3. This Act shall be in force from and after its passage.

CHAP. CCCXXVII.—*An Act to prevent the Arming and Equipping, within the jurisdiction of this State, of Vessels for Piratical or Privateering purposes, and other treasonable conduct.*—Approved April 25, 1863.

The People of the State of California,
represented in Senate and Assembly, do enact as follows:

SECTION 1. If any person shall, within the limits and jurisdiction of this State, fit out, arm, furnish, provide, or equip, or attempt to fit out, arm, furnish, provide, or equip, or procure to be fitted out, armed, furnished, provided, or equipped, or shall knowingly advise, or aid and abet, or be concerned in the fitting out, arming, furnishing, providing, or equipping, any private ship or vessel of war, or privateer, or vessel, sailing or intended to sail under any letter of marque, with intent that such ship or vessel shall be employed to cruise against or commit hostilities upon the citizens of the United States or their property, or if any person shall take the command of or enter on board any such ship or vessel, with the intent aforesaid, or shall purchase any interest in such ship or vessel, with the view to share the profits thereof, every such person so offending shall be deemed guilty of felony, and on conviction thereof, shall be punished by imprisonment in the State Prison for not more than twenty years nor less than five years, or shall suffer death ; *provided,* the jury by their verdict shall so determine and direct.

SEC. 2. If any person shall, within the limits and jurisdiction of this State, begin, or set on foot, or provide, or prepare, or furnish the means for, or knowingly aid and abet, or be concerned in beginning, setting on foot, or providing, preparing, or furnishing the means for any military or hostile expedition, to be carried on against the Government of the United States, or the loyal citizens thereof, or their property, every person so offending shall be deemed guilty of felony, and on conviction thereof, shall be punished by imprisonment in the State Prison not more than twenty years nor less than five years, or shall suffer death ; *provided,* the jury by their verdict shall so determine and direct.

SEC. 3. If any person shall, within the limits and jurisdiction of this State, enlist, or enter himself, or hire, or retain, or attempt to hire or retain another person to enlist himself, or aid, counsel, and advise, or aid and abet in procuring another to enlist himself as a soldier, or as a marine or sailor on board of any vessel, with intent that the person so enlisting shall commit hostilities against the Government or citizens of the United States, or their property, any person so offending shall be deemed guilty of felony, and on conviction thereof, shall be imprisoned in the State Prison not more than twenty years nor less than five years, or shall suffer death ; *provided,* the jury by their verdict shall so determine and direct.

SEC. 4. If any person shall accept, or deliver to another, any commission, or any letter of marque, purporting to emanate from or to be issued under the authority of the so-called Government of the Confederate States of America, with the intent that the same shall be used as a pretended authority to commit hostilities by land or sea against the Government of the United States, or the citizens thereof, or their property, every person so offending shall be deemed guilty of felony, and on conviction thereof, shall be punished by imprisonment in the State Prison for not more than twenty years and not less than five years, or shall suffer death ; *provided,* the jury by their verdict shall so determine and direct. The possession within this State of any such commission or letter of marque, shall be deemed *prima facie* evidence on the trial of such offender of the intent that the same shall be used as aforesaid.

SEC. 5. This Act shall take effect immediately.

CHAP. CCCLXV.—*An Act to exclude Traitors and Alien Enemies from the Courts of Justice in Civil Cases.*—Approved April 25, 1863.

The People of the State of California,
represented in Senate and Assembly, do enact as follows :

SECTION 1. Whenever any civil suit shall be pending in any Court of Record in this State, the defendant, or one of several defendants, or his Attorney, may, at any time after the commencement of the action, or the filing of the complaint therein, serve upon the plaintiff, if a natural person, or his attorney, a written notice, objecting to the further prosecution of said suit, on the ground of the disloyalty of the plaintiff; and thereupon all proceedings in said suit shall be stayed until said plaintiff shall take and subscribe, before some officer authorized to administer oaths, and shall file in said cause, an affidavit in the following form, to-wit:

" I [here insert the name of the plaintiff] do solemnly swear that I will support the Constitution of the United States and the Constitution of the State of California; that I will bear true faith and allegiance to the Government of the United States, any ordinance, resolution, or law of any State or Territory, or of any Convention or Legislature thereof, to the contrary notwithstanding; that I have not, since the [here insert the date of the passage of this Act] knowingly aided, encouraged, countenanced, or assisted, nor will I hereafter, in any manner, aid, encourage, countenance, or assist, the so-called Confederate States, or any of them, in their rebellion against the lawful Government of the United States; and this I do without any qualification or mental reservation whatsoever. So help me God."

And if the said plaintiff shall fail to take and file said oath within ten days after the giving of such notice, if a resident of the county, or within forty days, if a resident of the State and not of the county, or if not a resident of the State, then within such further reasonable time as the Court or a Judge thereof may determine, said case shall thereupon be absolutely dismissed, and no other suit shall ever be maintained by the said plaintiff, his grantees or assigns, for the same cause of action; *provided*, that the time may, for cause shown, be enlarged by the Court or a Judge thereof, and that the Court may relieve against any forfeiture or default arising from accident, surprise, or excusable neglect; and, *provided*, that where the plaintiff sues as a Trustee, or to the use of another, the oath may be taken by the person for whose benefit the action is prosecuted; and, further, *provided*, that when the plaintiff is a foreigner by birth, who has never been naturalized, nor declared his intention to become a citizen of the United States, he may take and file the following oath:

" I [inserting his name] do solemnly swear that I will not at any time, or in any manner, aid, encourage, countenance, or assist the so-called Confederate States, or any of them, in their rebellion against the Government of the United States, and that I will not, while a resident of the United States, knowingly commit or encourage any act tending to subvert the Constitution or Government thereof. So help me God."

SEC. 2. If a counter claim shall be set up, or new matter be affirmatively pleaded by the defendant in any suit, the plaintiff may, at any time after the filing of the anwer, give or cause to be given to the defendant, if a natural person or his Attorney, a similar notice to the one provided for in the preceding section, objecting, on like ground, to the introduction of such counter claim or affirmative matter; and thereupon, if the defendant shall fail to make and file a like oath, within the respective times in the said section above limited, such counter claim or new matter shall be disregarded by the Court, and the cause shall proceed as if the same had not been pleaded, and no suit shall ever be maintained by the said defendant, his grantees or assigns, for the same cause or matter.

SEC. 3. No Attorney at Law shall be permitted to practice in any Court in this State until he shall have taken and filed in the office of the County Clerk or the county in which the Attorney shall reside, the oath prescribed in this Act; and for every violation of the provisions of this section, the Attorney so offending shall be considered guilty of a misdemeanor, and on conviction, shall be fined in the sum of one thousand dollars.

SEC. 4. This Act, so far as the same relates to parties to an action, shall take effect immediately.*

CHAP. CCCCXCVIII.—*An Act to punish Offenses against the Peace of the State.*— Approved April 27, 1863.

The People of the State of California,
    represented in Senate and Assembly, do enact as follows:

SECTION 1. Every person who shall, in time of actual war waged against the United States, whether by a foreign or domestic foe, profess adherence to the common enemy, or, maliciously abusing the freedom of speech, shall publicly wish evil to the national cause, or that disaster may befall the national arms, or who shall in any manner rejoice at any reverse of the national army, or any part thereof, or who shall in any manner by word indorse, or defend, or cheer any overt attempt, or any person engaged in such overt attempt, to subvert and destroy the lawful authority of the United States in any State thereof, shall be deemed guilty of misdemeanor, and upon conviction thereof, shall be punished by imprisonment in the County Jail for a term not exceeding one year, or by a fine not exceeding one thousand dollars, or by both such fine and imprisonment.

Sections 28 and 29 of " An Act to provide for the Sale of certain Lands belonging to the State," passed April 27, 1863, read as follows :

SEC. 28. No location of land made under the provisions of this Act, or any proceedings in accordance therewith, shall be construed to give any title to, interest in, or right of possession or occupation of any of the Public Lands in this State, unless the person for whose benefit the location is made or the proceedings taken shall have first taken and subscribed the following oath or affirmation :

" I do solemnly swear [or affirm, as the case may be] that I will support, protect, and defend the Constitution and Government of the United States against all enemies, whether domestic or foreign, that I will bear true faith, allegiance, and loyalty to the said Constitution and Government, any ordinance or law of any State, Convention, or Legislature, or any rule or obligation of any society or association, or any decree or order from any source whatsoever, to the contrary notwithstanding ; and that I will support the Constitution of the State of California ; and further, that I do this with a full determination, pledge, and purpose, without any mental reservation or evasion whatsoever, and that this oath [or affirmation as the case may be] is not taken for the purpose of acquiring title to, interest in, or possession of any land in order that such title, interest, or possession may be transferred to any person or persons, to enable such person or persons to evade the provisions of any law of the State of California, or any regulation of the General Land Office at Washington."

SEC. 29. The certificate of the oath or affirmation prescribed in the preceding section shall be indorsed on a description of the land over which ownership or control is sought to be acquired, setting forth when the land had been surveyed by the General Government, the section and subdivision of section, township, and

---

* In *Wright* v. *Cohen*, the Supreme Court of California at its July Term, 1863, held the provisions of this Act, relating both to parties and attorneys, to be constitutional and valid Crocker J. delivered the opinion of the Court, Norton J. concurring.

range, in which such land is situated, and the said description, with the certificate of the oath or affirmation indorsed as prescribed by this section, shall be filed in the office of the Recorder of the county in which the land described is situated, and the right of the person making the oath or affirmation shall not be deemed to attach to such land by virtue of any proceedings under this act until the moment of the filing the description and certificate of the oath or affirmation in the office of the County Recorder, and no certificate of purchase or patent shall be issued to any person for lands located under this Act until a certified copy of said description and oath or affirmation has been filed in the office of the State Register.

DEBATE IN THE U. S. SENATE

UPON THE SECOND SECTION OF THE ACT OF JULY 17TH, 1862.

Mr. CLARK. The offense described in the second section is a new offense—the offense of inciting and setting on foot rebellion.

Mr. TRUMBULL. Or assisting it.

Mr. CLARK. Or assisting it in any way. It might amount to treason, or it might not.

Mr. TRUMBULL. How "not?"

Mr. CLARK. There may be a rebellion which may not amount to a levying of war. It may not be an armed rebellion. It may be an insurrection that does not amount to levying war. I do not say that it would be so in the case of the present rebellion. If a man is indicted for treason, I want the Court to have some discretion in regard to it, because it may turn out on the trial that there are circumstances mitigating it which the attorney who indicted him for treason did not know of. If there are none, let the Court inflict such punishment as they think he deserves. It certainly can do no harm, and may do a great deal of good.

Mr. TEN EYCK. It is of vast importance, as I understand the purport and effect of a recent decision of the Circuit Court of the United States for the Southern District of Ohio, where Judge Swayne has recently pronounced judgment quashing an indictment against certain persons who were indicted for aiding and assisting in this rebellion. The Court, in quashing the indictment, held that those words in the Constitution are solely applicable to aiding and assisting a foreign enemy, and do not apply to aid and assistance rendered now to persons in rebellion within the limits of the Union. Therefore these words in the second section, which give this new punishment for aiding and giving comfort to the existing rebellion, are of vast importance, and will cover all that class of cases which could not be reached under the decision of the Circuit Court in Ohio, as recently pronounced.

Mr. WADE. I do not understand that decision as the Senator from New Jersey does, although I have not seen more than a brief synopsis of it. Upon the first statement of it which I saw published, I understood it just as the Senator does; but I saw afterwards a little more detailed account of it, and I then perceived that the decision turned upon an entirely different point. In the first instance, I thought that the Judge intended to say that, in a civil war like the present, to aid, abet, or assist the enemy would not be treason under the Constitution; but on looking at the more detailed statement, I came to the conclusion that the decision turned entirely on the form of the indictment, and that the pleader, instead of having charged the man with having assisted and abetted the rebellion, ought to have charged him directly with levying war against the United States. The decision, as I understand it is, that in the case of a foreign war you may indict a man for giving aid and comfort to the enemy, but that in a domestic war your indictments must be under the other clause of the Constitution, and you must charge the man with levying war. It turns out that the decision was founded upon the mere technical form of pleading. The judgment of the Court was founded on a great number of English decisions, and it was that the indictment was vicious in not directly charging the defendant with having levied war, when the proof would have been that he aided and assisted the enemy that was levying war. That, I believe, is the amount of the decision.

Mr. Ten Eyck. It may be aside from the present discussion, but I certainly saw published in the *National Intelligencer* what purported to be a *verbatim* account of the opinion delivered by Justice Swayne; and the Court held that those words in our Constitution which make it treason to give aid and comfort to the enemy, were an exact copy of the old Norman-French, incorporated into an English statute, and cited several cases that had been decided in England under that very statute, holding that the treason therein spoken of consisted in giving aid and comfort to a foreign enemy, and could not and did not apply to giving aid and comfort to a rebellion within the realm. Although the Court may have said that the indictment was not sufficient, because it did not charge the actual levying of war, they held it so because of necessity it must have been so charged to hold the party indicted guilty of treason against the United States, for he could not be guilty of treason against the United States except under the first branch of the clause of the Constitution, which declares that "treason shall consist only in levying war against the United States, or adhering to their enemies, giving them aid and comfort." The Court held that treason consisted in levying war against the United States, but could not consist in giving aid and comfort to the citizens of the United States in rebellion against the Government. That is the decision upon which the Court quashed the indictment against a person whose name I do not remember: and under that decision Thomas B. Lincoln, who was the man that Bright was guilty of giving aid and comfort to, and others, go free.

Mr. Wade. I think the reason of that decision is this: in treason there are no accessories. If a man does anything to aid, abet, or assist, so that he would be an accessory before the fact in a felony, he becomes a principal traitor, and must be so treated in the indictment. It must, therefore, charge him directly with levying war, because that is the only treason in the case of a domestic war. The Court took a distinction between a domestic and a foreign war. Under these circumstances, the Judge said he was a principal traitor, and must be charged as such, because in treason there are no accessories. If a man is a traitor, if he assists at all, he is a principal traitor, and must be treated as such in an indictment, and that is all there was in the decision, as I understand it.

Mr. Davis. The same question that has been referred to in this debate was made before the District Court of the United States for Kentucky, and the District Judge there decided the law, as I understand it, in conformity to the decision of Chief Justice Marshall, and of the English Courts also. The clause in the Constitution which defines treason adopts, nearly literally, the language of the statute of 25 Edward III, and it gives two definitions of treason; one is levying war against the United States, and the other is adhering to the enemies of the United States, giving them aid and comfort. In the opinion rendered in the case of the *United States* v. *Chenowith*, decided by Judge Swayne, which has been referred to, it was ruled that the objection which was made to the indictment, and upon which it was quashed, might be obviated by the charge that the treasonable act was a levying of war; but here is the difficulty, as the Senator from Ohio well observed; there may be an adherence to the enemies of the United States and giving them aid and comfort, which is not an act of making war, and where that was the character of the aid and comfort given, of course it would be idle to charge against a party that he had levied war, for the proof being not that he had levied war, but that he had adhered to an enemy of the United States, giving him aid and comfort, and the act of adherence, and the aid and comfort given by him, not amounting to a levying of war, he could not be convicted. To my mind, two definitions of treason by the Constitution of the United States are palpable; and the distinction between an act of levying war and an act of adhering to the enemy of the United States, giving him aid and comfort, which might not be an act of making war, is plain and palpable. The English Courts in interpreting the Statute of 25 Edward III, and Chief Justice Marshall and the District Court of Kentucky, sustain this distinction, that where the proof amounted to the offense of adhering to an enemy, giving the enemy aid and comfort, and not the act of making war, that enemy must be a foreign State with which the United States was at war; and that an adherence to a domestic enemy was not an adherence to an enemy within the meaning of the Constitution, although aid and comfort were given that enemy, as would bring the party under the definition of the second branch of treason as defined by that instrument. In the case of the *United States* v. *Bollman*, the Court entered into a definition of what is an act of levying war, and decided some acts to be acts of levying war, and other acts not to be acts of levying war. These latter classes of acts might, and often would, be giving aid and comfort to the enemy, but they were not acts of the character that amounted to a levying of war. The principle decided by the English Courts and by the American Courts is, that where the act does not amount to a levying of war, but is an adherence to the enemy, giving the enemy aid and comfort, that act, to come within the last definition of treason by the Constitution, must be an adherence to a foreign enemy with which the United States are at war, giving that foreign enemy aid and comfort.

Mr. WADE. I desire to ask the Senator a question. If I understand him now correctly, it is no offense under any law of ours for a man to aid and assist the enemy, the rebels.

Mr. DAVIS. It is not treason.

Mr. WADE. Is it a punishable offense under our law?

Mr. DAVIS. I am not prepared to say whether it is or not.

Mr. WADE. I think the Senator is mistaken in supposing it is not treason. I do not think Judge Swayne so decided, but his decision referred to the form of the indictment.

Mr. DAVIS. I know that our District Judge so decided, and discharged men on that ground, very much against my inclination, but I thought his decision was right.

Mr. WADE. If that is so, it is a great defect which should be remedied.

Mr. DAVIS. I know that is the construction which the English Courts have given of the Statute of 25 Edward III, and my recollection is, that Chief Justice Marshall gave the same interpretation and construction to the clause of the Constitution of the United States in relation to treason.

*　　*　　*　　*　　*　　*　　*　　*　　*

Mr. WADE, It is impossible to a legal mind that there should be any difference between the crimes that are sought to be punished in the first and in the second sections of this bill. You ought not to punish the same offense differently in the same bill. I hardly know what the Judge may do under this bill. Under the first section he may take the life of a man, or he may fine and imprison him; and in the next section there is a different punishment altogether for the same offense. Now, let us see if it is not so. It will not be denied that the first section aims at the punishment of treason by name. Now, let us see if the offense described in the second section is not treason, whether it is so named or not. Let us see whether you can make anything else out of it:

" That if any person shall hereafter incite, set on foot, assist, or engage in any rebellion or insurrection against the authority of the United States, or the laws thereof, or shall give aid or comfort thereto, or shall engage in or give aid and comfort to any such existing rebellion or insurrection, and be convicted thereof—"

Convicted of what?

Mr. CLARK. Of aiding and inciting.

Mr. WADE. Very well. If you were a pleader, charging him with the offense, you would have to say he was guilty of treason, or else you could not make him guilty of anything. These facts amount to treason. Is it so that a man who incites, puts on foot, engages in an insurrection, is not a traitor?

Mr. CLARK. It may be.

Mr. WADE. No, sir, it cannot be so. He is a principal traitor. The man who aids, incites, abets, stirs up, or in any manner assists a rebellion is as much a principal traitor as he who goes to battle with arms in his hands. There is no difference between the first section and the second section as to the crime which each attempts to define. Both these sections aim to punish precisely the same thing, but with different punishments; and it would be an anomaly in law to have such an absurdity upon our statute book.　　*　　*　　*　　*　　*

*　　*　　*　　* The absurdity is that you undertake to make two different offenses out of one and precisely the same thing, and to affix different punishments for that which is the same. I do not think that a bill so vague, so indefinite, and with such a confusion of ideas running through it, ought to be permitted to go upon the statute book.

Mr. CLARK. I think that when the Senator considers the bill a little further, he will come to a different conclusion in regard to it. The first section imposes a punishment for the crime of treason. The crime is well defined. The section itself does not attempt to define it; but leaves it as it has been defined in the Constitution. The crime of treason is to be punished, according to the first section of this bill, by death, or by fine and imprisonment, and it requires two witnesses to the same overt act to convict a man. The second section prescribes a new offense; it is inciting, setting on foot, or engaging in rebellion or insurrection against the United States——

Mr. WADE. That is treason.

Mr. CLARK. It may be treason or it may not be treason. If the rebellion amounted to levying war, it would then become treason; but if not, it would not.

Now, the same distinction is preserved in the law in regard to murder and to man-slaughter. You may indict a man for murder, and if the facts brought out warrant a conviction you may punish him for murder. You may indict him for man-slaughter, and if the facts show that the crime was murder you cannot convict him of murder, because he is not charged with it. So here, if the attorney thinks the offense does not amount to more than inciting or setting on foot rebellion, he would charge him in the indictment with doing that thing, but not charge him with treason, and then, if the facts should come up to the charge, he would only be punished under this section. If the Senator desires that there should be some corporeal punishment under this section, as imprisonment, I have no objection to such an amendment; but the Senator, I think, will see on consideration that there is a clear distinction. You may convict the offender under the second section by one witness, because it does not amount to death. There may be cases where you cannot find more than one witness to the same overt act, where the man was clearly engaged in rebellion. You may convict him of the offense under the second section when you could not convict him of treason. Does not the Senator see that there is a clear distinction? For instance, in a case of burglary, break-ing, and entering, and stealing; you can convict of the stealing and charge the stealing when you abandon the burglarious intention. So here, we design that you may convict a man of being engaged in the rebellion when you abandon the charge of treason, if the facts do not amount to that in your opinion, so that the man shall be fined. The committee adopted this section for the purpose of bring-ing these men to trial, not simply for avoiding the distinction suggested by the Senator from New Jersey in regard to the decision of Judge Swayne, because on looking at that I am inclined to agree with the Senator from Ohio in regard to it. But there may be an insurrection and rebellion that does not amount to levying war, and there may be aiding it which does not amount to levying war.

Mr. HOWARD. I beg to make a single inquiry of my friend from New Hamp-shire, if he has no objection.

Mr. CLARK. Not the least.

Mr. HOWARD. I desire, now that he has the floor, that he will give us his ideas upon this point arising under the second section of the bill, whether, in his appre-hension, it creates more than one offense; and I wish him to have the goodness to explain the distinction between the various offenses therein created, if there are various offenses. It may have some importance in the course of the discussion.

Mr. CLARK. I do not apprehend that it creates more than one offense.

Mr. HOWARD. Very well.

Mr. CLARK. We did not intend that it should create more than one offense, and all to be punished alike.

Mr. HOWARD. Then I understand the Senator from New Hampshire sets up no distinction between inciting a rebellion or insurrection, setting on foot a rebell-ion or insurrection, assisting in a rebellion or insurrection, or engaging in a rebell-ion or insurrection. He regards all these acts as constituting one and the same offense. Do I understand him correctly?

Mr. CLARK. Certainly. We did not mean to multiply the offenses; but to give a description broad enough to bring the offender to trial. That was the design of the committee, that we should have a way of punishing this offense, and the com-mittee only designed to make the bill effective in that particular.

Mr. HARRIS. Mr. President, I am little surprised at, and it is with some regret that I observe, the manifest hostility of some of the avowed friends of a strong, efficient confiscation bill, to the provisions of the first section of this bill. It may not contain all that those Senators desire; yet, as it tends to accomplish their object, it seems to me that it would be better for them to allow it to pass, as, if not the best thing they can get, better than nothing.

It does not seem to me that these two sections, the first and second, are obnoxious to the criticisms which have been made upon them. The first section, as has been said by the chairman of the committee that reported the bill, provides for the punishment of treason—a crime defined by the Constitution. I concur entirely in the views expressed by the Senator from Kentucky on this point. As the law now stands, any person convicted of treason must be executed. Look at the case we have before us. Thousands, tens, hundreds of thousands of men, perhaps, have been guilty of that offense. Is it to be contemplated for a moment that all these men are to be indicted for treason and to be executed? No man in his senses can tolerate the idea. Some of them must be; some of them should be; but no man expects that ten thousand or a hundred thousand of these men will be indicted and executed; and yet we are, as the law now stands, shut up to that single punishment. I agree with the Senator from Kentucky, every man that has had much experience in criminal law knows that the great difficulty in punishing crime is, that the punishment is so severe that jurors will not do their duty.

This section, in my judgment, furnishes a judicious latitude for a Court in inflicting the punishment of treason. Let a man be convicted of treason, and it will be then for the Court in its sober judgment to decide what is the grade of his offense; has he been a leader; has he been one that has nourished, that has himself incited and led on this rebellion; is he one of its authors, one of its promoters; has he been for years engaged in preparing the mind of the southern people for it? If he has, let him be executed. Let there be a few signal, emphatic, striking examples of that kind; but who expects that all the traitors of the South shall be executed? This section, very wisely, in my judgment, provides for a class of traitors, those who will be convicted of treason, but will not be executed.

*   *   *   *   *   *   *   *   *

If the provision of this second section amounts to treason, the person accused will be convicted of treason. Any skillful prosecutor, any prosecutor who is fit to discharge the duties of a prosecutor, will indict under both sections, just as you indict a man for murder, and put a second count in the indictment for manslaughter. The indictment will be under both sections. There will be one count for treason, and there will be another count in the very language of the second section for the offense prescribed by that section, which would not have existed but for the section—a statutory offense. Whoever frames the indictment, and is fit to hold the office of public prosecutor, will frame his indictment in that way. Then, if the individual has been guilty of treason, he will be convicted under the first section; but if the Court should find any difficulty in making out upon the facts of the case, as they shall be proved before the jury, that it was treason, and it shall appear that it was something else, inciting rebellion or insurrection against the Government, the Court, of course, would instruct the jury to convict under the second section of that offense—a grievous offense to be sure, a very grave offense, but not an offense that amounted to treason under the Constitution.

Mr. HOWARD. Will the honorable Senator from New York allow me to ask him a question?

Mr. HARRIS. Certainly.

Mr. HOWARD. I ask whether the acts made criminal by the second section are not treason under the Constitution of the United States?

Mr. HARRIS. I am not prepared to say that they may not be, and I am not prepared to say that they are. I have not examined the decision of Judge Swayne; but if the views suggested by the Senator from New Jersey be correct, they might not amount to treason. At all events, there is no harm in making this provision so that if the Court shall hold that the conduct of a man brought in question upon an indictment for treason does not amount to treason, he shall not therefore be acquitted. You may provide a milder punishment for an offense that the Court do not deem to amount to treason, and thus you may punish the guilty individual, while he is at the same time acquitted of the crime of treason. There is no difficulty in the matter.

GENTLEMEN OF THE GRAND JURY:—The oath which has just
been administered to you indicates generally the nature of your
duties, and the impartial spirit with which those duties should be
discharged. You are impanneled to inquire into and true presentment make of all public offenses against the United States, committed or triable within the Northern Judicial District of California.
Your inquiries are to be conducted, and your presentments made,
without malice, hatred, or ill-will, and you are to leave no one unre-
sented through fear, favor, or affection, or for any reward, or the
promise or hope thereof. From the nature of the duties devolved
upon you, your office is one of responsibility, dignity, and importance. By the Constitution of the United States no person can " be
held to answer for a capital, or otherwise infamous crime, unless
on a presentment or indictment of a Grand Jury, except in cases
arising in the land or naval forces, or in the militia, when in actual service, in time of war or public danger." No steps, therefore, can be
taken for the prosecution of any crime of an infamous character—
and under that designation the whole series of felonies is classed—
beyond the warrant and commitment of the party accused, until the
Grand Jury have deliberated and acted upon the accusation. Your
functions are therefore not only important, but they are indispensable to the administration of justice.

In your investigations you will receive only legal evidence, to the
exclusion of mere reports, suspicions, and hearsay evidence. Subject to this qualification, you will receive all the evidence presented which may throw light upon the matter under consideration,

whether it tend to establish the innocence or the guilt of the accused. And, more : if in the course of your inquiries you have reason to believe that there is other evidence, not presented to you, within your reach which would qualify or explain away the charge under investigation, it will be your duty to order such evidence to be produced. Formerly, it was held that an indictment might be found if probable evidence was produced in support of the charge. But a different and more merciful rule now prevails. To justify the finding of an indictment, you must be convinced, so far as the evidence before you goes, that the accused is guilty; in other words, you ought not to find an indictment unless, in your judgment, the evidence before you, unexplained and uncontradicted, would warrant a conviction by a petit jury.[*]

The District Attorney has informed the Court that parties will be accused before you of offenses of the highest and gravest character ; some of treason against the United States ; some of enticing soldiers in the army of the United States to desert, and one of murder on the high seas. Upon the first of these offenses, the Court will proceed to give you some brief instructions.

Treason is defined by the Constitution of the United States. That instrument declares that " treason against the United States shall consist only in levying war against them, or in adhering to their enemies, giving them aid and comfort." The Constitution also provides that " the Congress shall have power to declare the punishment of treason." In 1790, in pursuance of the authority thus conferred, Congress passed an Act, of which the following is the first section : " If any person, or persons, owing allegiance to the United States of America, shall levy war against them, or shall adhere to their enemies, giving them aid and comfort within the United States or elsewhere, and shall be thereof convicted, on confession in open Court, or on the testimony of two witnesses to the same overt act of the treason whereof he or they shall stand indicted, such person or persons shall be adjudged guilty of treason against the United States, and shall suffer death." On the seventeenth of July, 1862, Congress passed another Act declaring that the punishment of treason, subsequently committed, shall be death, or fine and imprisonment, at the discretion of the Court,

---

* 1 Chitty's Crim. Law, 318.

and that the slaves of the party convicted, if any he have, shall be freed.

The Constitution, as you perceive, simply defines the crime of treason. The Act of 1790, in addition to declaring the punishment, also designates the persons by whom the crime may be committed ; " by any person or persons," it says, " owing allegiance to the United States." These terms neither enlarge nor restrict the sense of the provision, for treason can only be committed against the United States by those who owe allegiance to them. By allegiance is meant that fidelity and obedience which the individual owes to the Government in return for the protection which he receives. It may be absolute and permanent, or it may be qualified and temporary. The citizen owes allegiance permanently, or at least until, by some open and distinct act, he renounces it, and becomes a citizen or subject of another Government. The alien, whilst a resident within the United States, owes a qualified and temporary allegiance.* Enjoying the protection of the Government, he is bound by its laws during the period of his sojourn in the country. The Acts of Congress include all persons who owe any allegiance, whether it be of an absolute and permanent character, or of a qualified and temporary one. They embrace resident aliens as well as citizens.†

The words " levying war ", in the Constitution are not restricted to the act of making war for the entire overthrow of the Government, but embrace any combination to prevent, or oppose by force, the execution of a provision, either of the Constitution of the

---

* *United States* v. *Wietberger* (5 Wheat. 97.)

† East divides allegiance into *natural* and *local*. " Natural allegiance," he says, " is that which is due from every man who is born a member of the society. His birth in the State entitles him to peculiar privileges, which are with great propriety called his birthright ; and this being indefeasible, the allegiance arising out of it is equally unalienable ; it is due from him at all times and in all places." * * * * " Local allegiance is that which is due from a foreigner during his residence here ; and is founded in the protection he enjoys for his own person, his family, and effects, during the time of that residence. This allegiance ceases whenever he withdraws with his family and effects ; for his temporary protection being then at an end, the duty arising from it also determines. But if he only go abroad himself, leaving his family and effects here under the same protection, the duty still continues ; and if he commit treason, he may be punished as a traitor ; and this whether his own sovereign be at enmity or at peace with ours. Therefore, if he aid even his own countrymen in acts or purposes of hostility, while he is resident here, he may be dealt with in the same manner." (1 Pleas of the Crown, 50 and 52.)

United States or of any public statute of the United States, if accompanied or followed by an act of forcible opposition in pursuance of such combination. There must be a conspiracy to resist by force; there must be an assemblage of men to carry the treasonable purpose into effect; and there must be actual resistance by force, or intimidation by numbers. The conspiracy must be directed against the provision of the Constitution or law generally, and not to its application or enforcement in a particular case, or against a particular individual; in other words, the conspiracy must be to effect something of a *public nature*, as the overthrow of the Government, or a department thereof, or to nullify some law of the United States. To illustrate: A conspiracy to resist, by force of arms, the Conscription Law, in its application to a particular individual and actual resistance in pursuance of such conspiracy, would not constitute treason, though it would constitute an offense of a grave character. But if the conspiracy were to prevent the execution of the law generally, in all instances, and force were used pursuant to such conspiracy, there would be a case of levying war, and the conspirators would be guilty of treason.

You will have no difficulty in arriving at a correct conclusion, with reference to any particular case which may be brought to your attention, if you bear in mind that to constitute a levying of war there must be: *first*, an assemblage of persons in force—in a condition to make war; *second*, the assemblage must be for a treasonable purpose; *third*, there must be an actual use of force, or such display of numbers as to intimidate, in pursuance of such purpose. There must be the assemblage in force, the treasonable purpose, and the act accompanying or following it. A mere conspiracy to overthrow the Government either entirely, or as to one of its laws, or one of its departments, however atrocious, does not constitute the crime of treason. A conspiracy to levy war, and actually levying war, are distinct offenses.*

But when war is actually levied in any part of the country, any person, however far removed from the scene of military operations, who aids in its prosecution, is equally involved in the guilt of treason. "If war be actually levied," says Chief Justice Marshall,

---

* See Note A, Appendix.

" that is, if a body of men be actually assembled for the purpose of effecting by force a treasonable purpose, all those who perform any part, however minute, or however remote from the scene of action, and who are actually leagued in the general conspiracy, are to be considered as traitors."* War being levied, those actually engaged in open hostilities and those who adhere to them and supply them with money, arms, or munitions of war, are equally guilty of treason within the meaning of the constitutional provision.†

The Constitution has not only defined the crime of treason—it has prescribed a rule of evidence by which it shall be established. " No person," it declares, " shall be convicted of treason unless on the testimony of two witnesses to the same overt act, or on confession in open Court." By " overt act " is meant some conduct or movement on the part of the conspirators, in execution of the conspiracy. The terms embrace such acts as are visible—cognizable by the senses—as distinguished from mere dormant intention. And when the overt act is committed, the crime is consummated, even though the act fail to effect the object intended. Thus, where money or munitions of war are forwarded to those engaged in open hostilities, the overt act is committed, even though the money or munitions of war are intercepted before they reach their destination. So, if an expedition, whether by land or by sea, to aid or coöperate with the hostile parties, be fitted out within the jurisdiction of the United States, and it actually starts on its way, the crime is consummated though the expedition be arrested within the hour of its departure.‡

As no conviction can follow unless some overt act is established by the testimony of two witnesses, so no indictment ought to be found except upon like testimony.§

I have thus endeavored, gentlemen, to state to you, in as brief a manner as possible, the law with reference to treason. Until recently, the Courts of the United States have seldom been called upon to give any instructions as to this crime. Except within the last thirty months, the offense has been almost a stranger to our

---

* *Ex parte Bollman* and *Ex parte Swartwout* (4 Cranch. 126.)
† See Note B, Appendix.
‡ See Note C, Appendix.
§ See Note D, Appendix.

criminal calendars. But within this period a gigantic rebellion has arisen, aiming at nothing less than the overthrow of the Government, the division of the country, and the subversion of everything that has made the Republic great and honored among the nations.

In the efforts made to suppress this rebellion, and maintain the just authority of the Government, powers have been exercised which, except in a few instances, have lain dormant in the Constitution from the date of its adoption. Some of the parties against whom the charge of treason will be preferred before you, have been confined for months in one of our public forts, without process or judgment of any of the regular tribunals of the country. It is believed that they have been thus held under orders of the President, issued through the Department of War; and that with reference to them the writ of *habeas corpus* has been suspended. The Constitution contemplates that this writ may be suspended " when, in cases of rebellion or invasion, the public safety may require it. " In times of peace, a party arrested under process from the courts of justice, or a judicial officer, for an alleged public offense, is entitled to an examination without unnecessary delay; and if the charge be not sustained by evidence, he is discharged absolutely; and even if it be sustained, he is discharged, except in capital cases, conditionally—that is, upon giving bail. If after arrest an examination be not had, or if had, bail be not allowed, the accused can obtain his discharge or bail upon a writ of *habeas corpus*. It is plain that, by proceedings of this character, parties may be set at large whose detention, in times of rebellion or invasion, is imperatively demanded by the public safety. In such times arrests must often be made, not only for offenses already committed, but also when there is just apprehension that offenses are about to be committed; and it must sometimes happen, in both cases, that an examination would defeat the very object of the arrest. Take, for example, the case of a party arrested, upon whose person are found documents showing the plans, intended movements, resources, and negotiations of the insurgents, and implicating him in the general conspiracy. The proof of his guilt would be thus abundant; but it might well be that the Government would regard the information as too important for the public interests to be exposed by his examination before a judicial officer. In that view the Government would very properly hold him without an examination, by suspending the writ of *habeas corpus*. So a party might be arrested and an examination refused, because he was possessed of the secrets of our Government, which he was about to communicate to the enemy.

The Constitution guards with jealous care the liberty of the citizen. It provides that he shall be free from arrest except upon warrant issued upon probable cause, supported by oath or affirmation. But the Constitution was established not only for times of peace; not only for times when a ready obedience to the laws is yielded by citizens, but also for times of rebellion, of war and invasion, and it contains within itself all the power requisite for the maintenance of the Government against both foreign and domestic foes. The Government must exist, or the citizen cannot enjoy the liberty which the Constitution intends to secure. And that the Government may exist, the liberty of the individual must sometimes yield to the demands of public safety. The very clause of the Constitution which declares that the privilege of the writ of *habeas corpus* shall not be suspended makes the exception, " unless when, in cases of rebellion or invasion, the public safety may require it." *

---

* The following extract from the admirable letter of President Lincoln, of June 12th, 1863, to Erastus Corning and others—officers of a public meeting held at Albany—places this subject in a strong light :

" Ours is a case of rebellion—so called by the resolutions before me—in fact, a clear, flagrant, and gigantic case of rebellion ; and the provisions of the Constitution that "the privilege of the writ of *habeas corpus* shall not be suspended unless when, in cases of rebellion or invasion, the public safety may require it," is the provision which specially applies to our present case. This provision plainly attests the understanding of those who made the Constitution, that ordinary Courts of Justice are inadequate to "cases of rebellion"—attests their purpose that, in such cases, men may be held in custody whom the Courts, acting on ordinary rules, would discharge. *Habeas corpus* does not discharge men who are proved to be guilty of defined crime ; and its suspension is allowed by the Constitution on purpose that men may be arrested and held who cannot be proved to be guilty of defined crime, "when, in cases of rebellion or invasion, the public safety may require it." This is precisely our present case— a case of rebellion, wherein the public safety does require the suspension. Indeed, arrests by process of Courts, and arrests in cases of rebellion, do not proceed together altogether upon the same basis. The former is directed at the small per centage of ordinary and continuous perpetration of crime, while the latter is directed at sudden and extensive uprisings against the Government, which, at most, will succeed or fail in no great length of time. In the latter case arrests are made, not so much for what has been done, as for what probably would be done. The latter is more for the preventive and less for the vindictive than the former. In such cases the

An examination of a recent Act of Congress will exhibit the solicitude of the National Legislature, that the exercise of the power to suspend the writ of *habeas corpus*, so essential at times for the public safety, should be restrained by all possible guards against abuse. The act to which I refer was passed on the 3d of March, 1863, and is entitled, "An act relating to *habeas corpus*, and regulating judicial proceedings in certain cases." I will read to you its first three sections: [The Judge here read the sections.*]

By the first section of this act, as you perceive, Congress authorizes the President of the United States, during the present rebellion, whenever in his judgment the public safety may require it, to suspend the privilege of the writ in any case, throughout the United States or any part thereof. Whatever doubts may

---

purposes of men are much more easily understood than in cases of ordinary crime. The man who stands by and says nothing when the peril of his Government is discussed cannot be misunderstood. If not hindered he is sure to help the enemy; much more if he talks ambiguously—talks for his country with "buts" and "ifs" and "ands." Of how little value the constitutional provisions I have quoted will be rendered if arrests shall never be made until defined crimes shall have been committed, may be illustrated by a few notable examples. General John C. Breckinridge, General Robert E. Lee, General Joseph E. Johnston, General John B. Magruder, General William B. Preston, General Simon B. Buckner, and Commodore Franklin Buchanan, now occupying the very highest places in the rebel war service, were all within the power of the Government since the rebellion began, and were nearly as well known to be traitors then as now. Unquestionably, if we had seized and held them the insurgent cause would be much weaker. But no one of them had then committed any crime defined in the law. In view of these and similar cases, I think the time not unlikely to come when I shall be blamed for having made too few arrests rather than too many.

By the third resolution the people indicate their opinion that military arrests may be constitutional in localities where rebellion actually exists, but that such arrests are unconstitutional in localities where rebellion or insurrection does not actually exist. They insist that such arrests shall not be made "outside of the lines of necessary military occupation and the scenes of insurrection." Inasmuch, however, as the Constitution itself makes no such distinction, I am unable to believe that there is any such constitutional distinction. I concede that the class of arrests complained of can be constitutional only when, in cases of rebellion or invasion, the public safety may require them; and I insist that in such cases they are constitutional wherever the public safety does require them, as well in places to which they may prevent the rebellion extending as in those where it may be already prevailing; as well where they may restrain mischievous interference with the raising and supplying of armies to suppress the rebellion, as where the rebellion may actually be; as well where they may restrain the enticing men out of the army, as where they would prevent mutiny in the army; equally constitutional at all places where they will conduce to the public safety, as against the dangers of rebellion or invasion."

* See Note E, Appendix.

have been expressed as to the power of the President, as Commander-in-Chief of the army and navy, to suspend the writ without the previous authorization of Congress, there have been none as to the power of Congress to confer the authority in this respect.

But in order that the suspension of the writ may not be prolonged to the oppression of the citizen arrested, the second section of the act requires the Secretary of War and the Secretary of State to furnish, so soon as possible, a list of the persons held as state or political prisoners by order of the President or either of the Secretaries, to, the Judges of the Circuit and District Courts of the United States and of the District of Columbia; the list to contain the names of all persons thus held, who reside in the respective jurisdictions of the Judges, and the date of their arrest; and it declares that, in all cases where a Grand Jury has attended any of these Courts, having jurisdiction of the premises, after the passage of the act and the furnishing of the list, and has terminated its session without finding an indictment or presentment, or other proceeding against them, it shall be the duty of the Judges of said Courts, forthwith to make an order that any such persons, claiming a discharge from imprisonment, be brought before them to be discharged.

And lest the officer having such prisoners in his custody, holding them under the order of his superior, might refuse to obey the Judges in this respect, he is directed by the act to render immediate obedience to their orders, and in case of his delay or refusal to do so he is made liable to an indictment for a misdemeanor and may be punished by fine and imprisonment.

The only conditions which the Judges can impose, upon the discharge of a prisoner thus held, against whom no indictment is found, are that he shall take the oath of allegiance, and, if required, enter into a recognizance to keep the peace.

And lest the Secretaries of State and War may not furnish the list required by the previous provision, the third section declares that in case of their refusal or omission, for any reason, to furnish such list within twenty days after the passage of the act, as to prisoners then in custody, and within twenty days after their arrest as to prisoners thereafter arrested, any citizen may, after the Grand Jury has terminated its session without finding an indictment, by a petition alleging the facts, obtain an order for the discharge of the prisoners on the terms and conditions already mentioned.

It is hardly possible to conceive of greater checks against the abuse of the power which Congress has thus placed in the hands of the President. Even when the writ is suspended, in these times of war and insurrection, the detention of the prisoner can only extend to the meeting of the first Grand Jury of the Court having jurisdiction of the place where he is confined.

In the face of this statute, how unfounded, gentlemen, is the apprehension which is sometimes expressed, that the exercise by the President of the power vested in him is tending to the subversion of our liberties. Whilst the Government is making extraordinary efforts to crush and destroy a gigantic rebellion, it would be far more loyal and patriotic if parties, instead of endeavoring to weaken and embarrass its efforts, by unfounded and calumnious accusations, would labor to strengthen its hands in every way possible.

The Act of Congress of 1790, to which reference has already been made, in its second section defines the crime of misprision of treason. The section is as follows:

" If any person or persons, having knowledge of the commission of any of the treasons aforesaid, shall conceal and not as soon as may be disclose and make known the same to the President of the United States, or some one of the Judges thereof, or to the President or Governor of a particular State, or some one of the Judges or Justices thereof, such person or persons, on conviction, shall be adjudged guilty of misprision of treason, and shall be imprisoned not exceeding seven years and fined not exceeding one thousand dollars."

If, therefore, any persons have knowledge that acts of treason have been committed within this district, it is their duty to disclose the same to the proper authorities, and where such acts have been concealed the matter will be a suitable subject for your investigation.

The other cases which may be brought before you do not require any special instructions from the Court. The District Attorney of the United States will always be ready to furnish you such information as may be necessary to aid you in your inquiries.

The jury then retired to deliberate.

APPENDIX.

The clause in the Constitution was taken from the Statute of the 25 Edw. III, St. 5, C. 2, called the Statute of Treasons. By that statute it is declared to be high treason "when a man doth compass or imagine the death of our Lord the King, or of our Lady his Queen, or of their eldest son and heir; or if a man do violate the King's companion, or the King's eldest daughter unmarried, or the wife of the King's eldest son and heir; *or if a man do levy war against our Lord the King in his realm, or be adherent to the King's enemies in his realm, giving to them aid and comfort in the realm or elsewhere;* and thereof be provably attainted of open deed by the people of their condition; and if a man counterfeit the King's great or privy seal, or his money; and if a man bring false money into this realm, counterfeit to the money of England, as the money called Lushburgh, or other like to the said money of England, knowing the money to be false, to merchandize or make payment, in deceit of our Lord the King and his people; and if a man slay the Chancellor, Treasurer, or the King's justices of the one bench or the other, Justices in Eyre, or Justices of Assize, and all other justices assigned to hear and determine, being in their places doing their offices."

" The levying war" says East, in commenting upon the above statute, "is either express and direct, or constructive. Of the first sort are all insurrections against the person of the King, whether they be to dethrone, imprison, or force him to alter his measures of Government, or to remove evil counsellors from about him. In *Essex's Case*, though the indictment was upon the clause of compassing the Queen's death, yet, says Lord Hale, his riding armed into London, and soliciting the citizens to go with him to court to remove the Queen's ministers, and his fortifying his house against the Queen's officers, were in truth overt acts of levying war. So the attacking the King's forces, in opposition to his authority, upon a march or in quarters, is levying war against the King. But if, upon a sudden quarrel, from some affront given or taken, and not as a cover for any traitorous design, the neighborhood should rise and drive the King's forces out of their quarters; though it would be a great misdemeanor, and, if death ensued, might be felony in the assailants; yet, it will not be a treason; there being no intention against the King's person or Government." (1 Pleas of the Crown, 66.) * * * It must in general be difficult in the inception of intestine troubles to fix the period when opposition to the established Government shall be said to wear the formidable appearance of insurrection, and to constitute what in the terms of the act is called a levying of war against the King. It is strictly, therefore, a question of fact to be tried by the jury under all the circumstances. Any assembly of persons, met for a treasonable purpose, armed and arrayed in a warlike manner, is *bellum levatum*, though not *percussum*. Enlisting and marching are sufficient overt acts, without coming to an actual engagement; in the same manner as cruising under an enemy's commission, though no act of express hostility be proved, is an adherence to the King's enemies. (Id. 67.) * * * * "Holding a castle or fort against the King or his troops, if actual force be used in order to keep possession, is levying war." (Id. 68.) * * * * "Joining with rebels, freely and voluntarily, in any act of rebellion, is levying war against the King." (Id. 70.) * * * * "So sending money, arms, ammunition, or other necessaries to rebels, will *prima facie* make a man a traitor, though they should be intercepted. (Id. 72.) * * * *

"Constructive levying of war is in truth more directed against the Government than the person of the King; though, in legal construction, it is a levying of war against the King himself. This is when an insurrection is raised to reform some national grievance, to alter the established law or religion, to punish magistrates, to introduce innovation of a public concern, to obstruct the execution of some general law by an armed force, or for any other purpose, which usurps the Government in matters of a public and general nature. On the trial of Lord George Gordon, the Court of King's Bench declared their unanimous opinion, that an attempt by intimidation and violence to force the repeal of a law, was a levying war against the King." (Id. 72.) * * * * "But where the object of the insurrection is a matter of a private or local nature, affecting, or supposed to affect, only the parties assembled, or confined to particular persons or districts, it will not amount to high treason, although attended with the circumstances of military parade, usually alleged in the indictments on this branch of treason. As if the rising be only against a particular market, or to destroy particular inclosures, to remove a local nuisance, to release a particular prisoner, unless imprisoned for high treason, or even to oppose the execution of an Act of Parliament, if it only affect the district of the insurgents; as in the case of the Turnpike Act." (Id. 75.) * * * * "By the term enemy, is always to be understood a foreign power owing no allegiance to the Crown, and in a state of open hostility with us, though, perhaps, war may not have been regularly declared between the respective countries; and therefore, in an indictment on this clause, it is sufficient to aver, that the Prince or State adhered to, *was an enemy*. And the question, whether there be war or not between such power and our King, is purely a question of fact, triable by the jury; and public notoriety is sufficient evidence of it." (Id. 77.) * * * * "In considering what shall be deemed an adherence to the King's enemies, much of what has been already said under the head of levying war, is equally applicable. Thus, every species of aid or comfort, in the words of the statute, which, when given to a rebel within the realm, would make the subject guilty of levying war; if given to an enemy, whether within or without the realm, will make the party guilty of adhering to the King's enemies; though the case of giving aid to enemies within the realm, a subject might in some instances be brought within both branches of the act." (Id. 78.)

Mr. Chief Justice Marshall, in an opinion delivered in the progress of the trial of Aaron Burr, in considering the import of the words " levying war," said : " Had their first application to treason been made by our Constitution, they would certainly have admitted of some latitude of construction. Taken most literally, they are perhaps of the same import with the words raising or creating war; but as those who join after the commencement are equally the objects of punishment, there would probably be a general admission that the term also comprehended making war or carrying on war. In the construction which Courts would be required to give these words, it is not improbable that those who should raise, create, make, or carry on war, might be comprehended."

" The various acts, which would be considered as coming within the term, would be settled by a course of decisions; and it would be affirming boldly to say that those only who actually constituted a portion of the military force appearing in arms could be considered as levying war. There is no difficulty in affirming that there must be a war or the crime of levying it cannot exist; but there would often be considerable difficulty in affirming that a particular act did or did not involve the person committing it in the guilt and in the fact of levying war. If, for example, an army should be actually raised for the avowed purpose of carrying on open war against the United States and subverting their Government, the point must be weighed very deliberately before a Judge would venture to decide that an overt act of levying war had not been committed by a commissary of purchases, who never saw the army, but who, knowing its object and leaguing himself with the rebels, supplied that army with provisions ; or by a recruiting officer holding a commission in the rebel service, who, though never in camp, executed the particular duty assigned to him." (2 Burr's Trial, 402.)

Judge Iredell, of the Supreme Court, in his charge to the Grand Jury in the Circuit Court, held in the City of Philadelphia in April, 1799, referring particularly to the resistance by the Northampton insurgents to the enforcement of the Land Tax Act, said : " The only species of treason likely to come before you is that of levying war against the United States. There have been various opinions, and different determinations, on the import of those words. But I think I am warranted in saying, that if, in the case of the insurgents who may come under your consideration, the intention was to prevent by force of arms the execution of any Act of the Congress of the United States altogether (as, for instance, the Land Tax Act, the object of their opposition), any forcible opposition calculated to carry that intention into effect, was a levying of war against the United States, and of course an act of treason. But if the intention was merely to defeat its operation in a particular instance, or through the agency of a particular officer, from some private or personal motive, though a higher offense may have been committed, it did not amount to the crime of treason. The particular motive must, however, be the sole ingredient in the case, for if combined with a general view to obstruct the execution of the Act, the offense must be deemed treason." (Wharton's State Trials, 480.)

Judge Chase, of the Supreme Court, in his charge to the jury on the second trial of John Fries for treason, in April, 1800, said : " The Court are of opinion, that if a body of people conspire and meditate an insurrection to resist or oppose the execution of any statute of the United States by force, that they are only guilty of a high misdemeanor; but if they proceed to carry such intention into execution by force,' that they are guilty of the treason of levying war, and the quantum of the force employed neither lessens nor increases the crime—whether by one hundred, or one thousand persons, is wholly immaterial.

"The Court are of opinion, that a combination or conspiracy to levy war against the United States is not treason, unless combined with an attempt to carry such combination or conspiracy into execution; some actual force or violence must be used, in pursuance of such design to levy war; but that it is altogether immaterial whether the force used is sufficient to effectuate the object—any force, connected with the intention, will constitute the crime of levying war." (Id. 634.)

Judge Story, of the Supreme Court, in a charge to the Grand Jury of the Circuit Court of the United States, at Newport, in June, 1842, said: "To constitute an actual levy of war, there must be an assembly of persons, met for the treasonable purpose, and some overt act done, or some attempt made by them with force to execute, or towards executing, that purpose. There must be a present intention to proceed in the execution of the treasonable purpose by force. The assembly must now be in a condition to use force, and must intend to use it, if necessary, to further, or to aid, or to accomplish the treasonable design. If the assembly is arrayed in a military manner—if they are armed and march in a military form, for the express purpose of overawing or intimidating the public—and thus they attempt to carry into effect the treasonable design—that will, of itself, amount to a levy of war, although no actual blow has been struck, or engagement has taken place. This is a clear case; but it is by no means the only case (for many others might be stated) in which there may be an actual overt act of levying war. I wish to state this only as one case, upon which no doubt whatsoever can be entertained.

"In respect to the treasonable design, it is not necessary that it should be a direct and positive intention entirely to subvert or overthrow the Government. It will be equally treason, if the intention is by force to prevent the execution of any one or more general and public laws of the Government, or to resist the exercise of any legitimate authority of the Government in its sovereign capacity. Thus, if there is an assembly of persons with force, with an intent to prevent the collection of the lawful taxes, or duties, levied by the Government—or to destroy all Custom Houses—or to resist the administration of justice in the Courts of the United States, and they proceed to execute their purpose by force—there can be no doubt, that it would be treason against the United States." (1 Story, 614.)

Judge Curtis, of the Supreme Court, in his charge to the Grand Jury, in Boston, October 15th, 1851, said: "This crime (treason) is defined by the Constitution itself, and its magnitude, as well as the importance of a fit and rigid definition of it, may be inferred from the fact, that it is the only offense defined by that instrument. It is there made to consist in levying war against the United States, or adhering to their enemies, giving them aid and comfort. This language is borrowed from an ancient English statute, enacted in the year 1352, (25 Ed. III) mainly for the purpose of restraining the power of the Crown to oppress the subject by arbitrary constructions of the law of treason. At the time of the introduction of this language into our Constitution, it had acquired a settled meaning, and that meaning has been adopted by the Courts of the United States when they had occasion, as unfortunately they have had occasion, to interpret these words. This settled interpretation is, that the words 'levying war,' include not only the act of making war for the purpose of entirely overturning the Government, but also any combination forcibly to oppose the execution of any public law of the United States, if accompanied or followed by an act of forcible opposition to such law in pursuance of such combination. The following elements, therefore, constitute this offense :

" 1. A combination, or conspiracy, by which different individuals are united in one common purpose.

" 2. This purpose being to prevent the execution of some public law of the United States by force.

" 3. The actual use of force, by such combination, to prevent the execution of that law.

" These elements require some further explanation, to prevent their true nature from being misunderstood. It is not enough that the purpose of the combination is to oppose the execution of a law *in some particular case*, and in that only.

"If a person, against whom process has issued from a Court of the United States, should assemble and arm his friends forcibly, to prevent an arrest, and in pursuance of such design resistance should be made by those thus assembled, they would be guilty of a very high crime, but it would not be treason, if their combination had reference solely *to that case*. But if process of arrest issue under a law of the United States, and individuals assemble, forcibly to prevent an arrest under such process, pursuant to *a design* to prevent any person *from being arrested under that law*, and with such intent, force is used by them for that purpose, they are guilty of treason." (2 Curtis, 633, 634.) "Such a conspiracy may be formed before the individuals assemble to act, and they may come together to act pursuant to it; or, it may be formed when they have assembled, and immediately before the act. The time is not essential. All that is necessary, is, that being assembled, they should act in forcible opposition to a law of the United States, pursuant to a common design to prevent the execution of that law, in any case within their reach. Actual force must be used. But what amounts to the use of force, depends much upon the nature of the enterprise, and the circumstances of the case." (Id. 635.)

Judge Kane, of the District Court of the Eastern District of Pennsylvania, in a charge to a Grand Jury on the law of treason, in April, 1851, said ; " The expression 'levying war,' so regarded, embraces not merely that act of formal or declared war, but any combination forcibly to prevent or oppose the execution or enforcement of a provision of the Constitution, or of a public statute, if accompanied or followed by an act of forcible opposition in pursuance of such combination. This, in substance, has been the interpretation given to these words by the English Judges, and it has been uniformly and fully recognized and adopted in the Courts of the United States.

" The definition, as you will observe, includes two particulars, both of them indispensable elements of the offense. There must have been a combination or conspiring together to oppose the law by force, and some actual force must have been exerted, or the crime of treason is not consummated.

"The highest, or at least the direct proof of the combining, may be found in the declared purposes of the individual party before the actual outbreak; or it may be derived from the proceedings of meeting, in which he took part openly, or which he either prompted, or made effective, by his countenance or sanction,— commending, counseling, or instigating, forcible resistance to the law. I speak, of course, of a conspiring to resist a law, not the more limited purpose to violate it, or to prevent its application and enforcement in a particular case, or against a particular individual. The combination must be directed against the law itself.

"But such a direct proof of this element of the offense is not legally necessary to establish its existence. The concert of purpose may be deduced from the concerted action itself, or it may be inferred, from facts concurring at the time, or afterward, as well as before.

"Besides this, there must be some act of violence, as the result or consequence of the combining. But here, again, it is not necessary to prove that the individual accused, was a direct, personal actor in the violence. If he was present, directing, aiding, abetting, counseling, or countenancing it, he is in law guilty of the forcible act. Nor is even his personal presence indispensable. Though he be absent at the time of its actual perpetration, yet if he directed the act, devised or knowingly furnished the means, for carrying it into effect, instigating others to perform it, he shares their guilt. In treason, there are no accessories." (2 Wallace, 136.)

Judge Greer, of the Supreme Court of the United States, in his charge to the jury, in the case of the *United States* v. *Hanway*, in 1851, expressed his concurrence in the views contained in the above charge of Judge Kane. (Id. 204.) He also said: "What constitutes 'levying war' against the Government, is a question which has been the subject of much discussion, whenever an indictment has been tried under this article of the Constitution. The offense is described in very few words, and in their application to particular cases, much difference of opinion may be expected. We derive our laws as well as our language from England. As we would apply to the English dictionaries and classical writers, to ascertain the proper meaning of a particular word, so when we would inquire after the true definition of certain legal phraseology, we would naturally look to the text writers and judicial decisions which we know that the framers of our Constitutions would regard as the standard authorities in questions of legal definition. Otherwise, the language of the Constitution on this subject might be subject to any construction which the passion or caprice of a Court and jury might choose to give it in times of public excitement. At one time the Constitution might be nullified by a narrow construction, and at another time the life and liberty of the citizen be sacrificed by a latitudinous one." (2 Wallace, 200.) And again: "Since the adoption of the Constitution, but few cases of indictment for treason have occurred, and most of them not many years afterwards. Many of the English cases, *then* considered good law, and quoted by the best text writers as authorities, have since been discredited, if not overruled, in that country. The better opinion there at present seems to be, that the term 'levying war,' should be confined to insurrections and rebellions for the purpose of overturning the Government by force and arms. Many of the cases of constructive treason, quoted by Foster, Hale, and other writers, would perhaps now be treated merely as aggravated riots or felonies." (Id. 201.)

[NOTE B.]

Judge Curtis in his charge to the Grand Jury in 1851 already referred to said : " It should be known also, that treason may be committed by those not personally present at the immediate scene of violence. If a body of men be actually assembled to effect by force a treasonable purpose, all those who perform any part, however minute, or however remote from the scene of action, and who are actually leagued in the general conspiracy, are to be considered guilty of treason.

Influential persons cannot form associations to resist the law by violence, excite the passions of ignorant and unreflecting, or desperate men, incite them to action, supply them with weapons, and then retire and await in safety the result of the violence which they themselves have caused. To permit this, would not only be inconsistent with sound policy, but with a due regard to the just responsibilities of men. The law does not permit it. They who have the wickedness to plan and incite and aid, and who perform any part however minute, are justly deemed guilty of this offense, though they are not present at the immediate scene of violence." (2 Curtis, 635.)

———

" It is now too well settled to admit of question, that the law knows no accessories in treason; but that every one who, if it were a felony, would be an accessory, is, in the law of treason, a principal traitor. This rule, being now a constituent part of the law of treason, as administered in this country ever since its settlement, and in England for several centuries, its origin and history are of no importance. It is sufficient for us, that it is a part of the law of the land; and whatever may have been the reason on which it was originally founded, its high expediency, not to say necessity, for the prevention of this greatest of crimes, amply justifies its retention as a rule of law.

We are well aware that, in *Burr's Case*, this point was discussed before Marshall, C. J., and that he declined giving any opinion, because the case did not absolutely require it; and that, so far as the bias of his mind can be discovered, he seemed to doubt its application, in trials for treason against the United States, on the ground that the national tribunals could take no jurisdiction of crimes, under the common law; though he, at the same time, admitted that it was a sound rule of the law of treason against a single State. But it is to be observed, that when the Constitution or statutes of the United States give to their Courts jurisdiction over a crime, known to the common law, this law may always be consulted for the definition, extent, and attributes of that particular crime, where the statute is silent on the subject. These Courts cannot assume jurisdiction of crimes, merely on the basis of the common law. Their jurisdiction must be given by express statute or the Constitution; but, when given, the nature and extent of the authority may be ascertained by reference to the common law. To this extent the Courts seem to have agreed. (See *United States* v. *Coolidge*, 1 Gall. 488 ; *United States* v. *Hudson*, 7 Cranch, 32 ; Wilson's Works, vol. 3, pp. 371, 377 ; Duponceau on Jurisdiction, *passim;* 1 Kent's Com. Lect. 16, pp. 331, 341.) Now the Constitution makes it treasonable to levy war, but does not define the offense, nor describe the persons who may be said to have committed it. The common law does both; and is therefore to be resorted to for this knowledge. It says that every person, doing an act in regard to levying war, which, in a case of felony would render him an accessory before the fact, is guilty of the treason of levying war.

In the trial of John Fries, Mr. Justice Chase, in his charge to the jury, said that " in treason, all the *participes criminis* are principals; there are no accessories to this crime. Every act which, in the case of felony, would render a man an accessory, will, in the case of treason, make him a principal." (Fries' Trial, page 198.) No exception was taken to this position by the learned gentlemen who watched for the prisoner's safety, though they declined to assist him during the trial; nor is it known to have been impugned by any contrary decision.

It only remains then to ascertain what constitutes an accessory before the fact. And such is he who, being absent at the time of the felony committed, does yet procure, counsel, or command another to commit a felony. Words amounting to a bare permission will not alone constitute this offense; neither will a mere concealment of the design to commit a felony. It is not necessary, to this degree of crime, that the connection between the accessory and the actor be immediate; for if one procures another to cause some third person to commit a felony, and he does so, the procurer is accessory before the fact, though he never saw or heard of the individual finally employed to commit the crime. (See Wharton's Amer. Crim. Law, pp. 33, 36; 1 Hale, P. C., 613, 615; Idem., 374; 2 Hawk, P. C., ch. 29, sec. 16, *Rex* v. *Soares*, Russ & Ry. 25; *The People* v. *Norton*, 8 Cowen, 137; Foster's Cr. L. 125, 126; *McDaniel's Case*, 19 How. St. Tr. 804; *Earl of Somerset's Case*, 2 How. St. Tr. 965.) Where the principal acts under instructions from the accessory, it is not necessary, in order to affect the latter, that the instructions be proved to have been precisely followed; it will be sufficient if it be shown that they have been substantially complied with. Thus, if one instructs another to commit a murder by poison, and he perpetrates it with a sword, the former is accessory to the murder, for that was the substance of the instruction. So if the person employed goes beyond his instructions, in the circumstances of the transaction—as if he be instructed to rob, and in so doing he kills the victim; or if he be instructed to burn the house of A, and in so doing the flames extend to the house of B—the person counseling and directing the act is accessory to the murder, and to the second arson, for the latter was the probable consequence of the former; and every man is presumed to foresee and assume the probable consequences of his own acts. So if the party employed to commit a felony on one person, perpetrates it by mistake on another, the party counselling is accessory to the crime actually committed. It is only when the actor totally and substantially departs from his instructions that he stands alone in the offence. (See Foster's Cr. L. 369, 370, 372; 1 Hale, P. C. 616–618; 1 Russ on Crimes, 35, 36; Whart. Amer. Crim. L. pp. 34, 35.)

Upon these principles it is that every one who counsels, commands, or procures others to commit an overt act of treason, which is accordingly committed, is himself liable to the penalty of the law, as a principal traitor.

We have been thus particular in stating the law of treason, for the especial benefit of that class of persons who counsel, advise, incite, and procure others forcibly to resist the law of the land, in any and every instance in which its execution may be attempted, and it is accordingly forcibly resisted. Whether clerical or laymen, orthodox or heterodox, editors of newspapers, or lyceum lecturers, Northmen or Southrons, whoever or whatever they be, thus doing, they are guilty of treason." (The Monthly Law Reporter of December, 1851.)

[NOTE C.]

" Furnishing rebels or enemies with money, arms, ammunition, or other necessaries, will, *prima facie*, make a man a traitor. But if enemies or rebels come with a superior force and exact contributions, or live upon the country at free quarter, submission in these cases is not criminal ; for *flagrante bello* the *jus belli* taketh place it is the only law there subsisting; and submission is a point of the highest prudence to prevent a greater public evil.

And the bare sending money or provisions (except in the case just excepted), or sending intelligence to rebels or enemies, which in most cases is the most effectual aid that can be given them, will make a man a traitor, though the money or intelligence should happen to be intercepted ; for the party in sending did all he could ; the treason was complete *on his part, though it had not the effect he intended.*" (Foster's Crown Law, 217.)

[NOTE D.]

In his charge to the Grand Jury, in 1797, already referred to, Judge Iredell said : " With regard to the number of witnesses in treason, I am of opinion that two are necessary on the indictment as well as upon the trial in court. The provision in the Constitution, that the two witnesses must be to the same overt act (or actual deed constituting the treasonable offense), was in consequence of a construction which had prevailed in England, that though two witnesses were required to prove an act of treason, yet if one witness proved one act and another witness another act of the same species of treason (as for instance that of levying war), it was sufficient, a decision which has always appeared to me contrary to the true intention of the law which made two witnesses necessary—this provision being, as I conceived, intended to guard against fictitious charges of treason, which an unprincipled government might be tempted to support and encourage, even at the expense of perjury, a thing much more difficult to be effected by two witnesses than one." (Wharton's State Trials, 480.)

Judge Cadwallader, of the District Court of the Eastern District of Pennsylvania, is of a different opinion on this point. In the case of the *United States* v. *Greiner*, he said :

" The evidence for the prosecution has consisted of the direct testimony of one witness to the alleged overt act, and of admissions made voluntarily by the accused party since his arrest. The Constitution provides that no person shall be *convicted* of treason unless on the testimony of two witnesses to the same overt act, or on confession in open court. The admissions here proved were not such confessions, and, upon the trial of an indictment, would not in connection with the testimony of the single witness to the overt act suffice to warrant a conviction. But the provision of the Constitution and the language of the first section of the Act of April 30th, 1790 (1790, ch. 9, §1, 1 Stat. at Large, 112), on the subject, apply only to the trial of indictments, and are inapplicable to proceedings before Grand Juries, or to preliminary investigations like the present.

This appears to have been the opinion of Chief Justice Marshall (1 Burr's Tr. 196), and likewise of my judicial predecessor in this district (2 Wall. Jr. 138). Judge Iredell had, indeed, been previously of a different opinion (1 Whart. St. Tr. 480). His impression had probably been derived from the opinions which, under the statutes, 1 Edward VI, c. 12, s. 22; 5 Edward VI, c. 11, s. 11, and 7 W. 3, c. 3, had prevailed in England. See *Fenwick's Case* (13 State Trials, 537, and 26 How. 731.) As the point has never been directly decided in the United States, it may not be amiss to mention a difference between the language of the English statutes and the words of the Constitution. Those statutes enacted that no person should be *indicted*, or convicted of treason, unless, etc. The Constitution, omitting the word "indicted," uses the single word "convicted." This difference in language to which the attention of Chief Justice Marshall was doubtless directed, though he does not mention it, seems to be decisive of the question. The intention of the framers of the Constitution must have been to restrain the application of the prescribed rule of evidence to the trial of the indictment. A person should not, however, be indicted or imprisoned under a charge of treason when there is no rational probability that the charge, if true, can be proved by two witnesses on the future trial." (The Monthly Law Reporter, of May, 1861.)

[NOTE E.]

The first three sections of the Act of Congress, entitled "An Act relating to Habeas Corpus, and regulating Judicial Proceedings in certain cases," approved March 3d, 1863.

Be it enacted by the Senate and House of Representatives of the United States of America, in Congress assembled, That during the present rebellion the President of the United States, whenever, in his judgment, the public safety may require it, is authorized to suspend the privilege of the writ of *habeas corpus* in any case throughout the United States or any part thereof. And whenever and wherever the said privilege shall be suspended as aforesaid, no military or other officer shall be compelled, in answer to any writ of *habeas corpus*, to return the body of any person or persons detained by him by authority of the President; but upon the certificate, under oath, of the officer having charge of any one so detained, that such person is detained by him as a prisoner under authority of the President, further proceedings under the writ of *habeas corpus* shall be suspended by the Judge or Court having issued the said writ, so long as said suspension by the President shall remain in force, and said rebellion continue.

SEC. 2. *And be it further enacted,* That the Secretary of State and the Secretary of War be and they are hereby directed, as soon as may be practicable, to furnish to the Judges of the Circuit and District Courts of the United States, and of the District of Columbia, a list of the names of all persons, citizens of States, in which the administration of the laws has continued unimpaired in the said Federal Courts, who are now, or may hereafter be, held as prisoners of the United States, by order or authority of the President of the United States or either of said Secretaries, in any fort, arsenal, or other place, as State or political prisoners, or otherwise than as prisoners of war; the said list to contain the names of all those who reside in the respective jurisdictions of said Judges, or who may be deemed by the said Secretaries, or either of them, to have violated any law of the United States in any of said jurisdictions, and also the date of each arrest; the Secretary of State to furnish a list of such persons as are imprisoned by the order or authority of the President, acting through the State Department, and the Secretary of War a list of such as are imprisoned by the order or authority of the President, acting through the Department of War. And in all cases where a Grand Jury, having attended any of said Courts having jurisdiction in the premises, after the passage of this Act, and after the furnishing of said list, as aforesaid, has terminated its session without finding an indictment or presentment, or other proceeding against any such person, it shall be the duty of the Judge of said Court forthwith to make an order that any such prisoner desiring a discharge from said imprisonment be brought before him to be discharged; and every officer of the United States having custody of such prisoner is hereby directed immediately to obey and execute said Judge's order; and in case he shall delay or refuse so to do, he shall be subject to indictment for a misdemeanor, and be punished by a fine of not less than five hundred dollars and imprisonment in the common jail for a period not less than six months, in the discretion of the Court; *provided*, however, that no person shall be discharged by virtue of the provisions of this Act until after he or she shall have taken an oath of allegiance to the Government of the United States, and to support the Constitution thereof; and that he or she will not hereafter in any way encourage or give aid and comfort to the present rebellion, or the supporters thereof; and *provided*, also, that the Judge or Court before whom such person may be brought, before discharging him or her from imprisonment, shall have power, on examination of the case, and, if the public safety shall require it, shall be required to cause him or her to enter into recognizance, with or without surety, in a sum to be fixed by said Judge or Court, to keep the peace and be of good behavior toward the United States and its citizens, and from time to time, and at such times as such Judge or Court may direct, appear before said Judge or Court to be further dealt with according to law, as the circumstances may require. And it shall be the duty of the District Attorney of the United States to attend such examination before the Judge.

SEC. 3. *And be it further enacted*, That in case any such prisoners shall be under indictment or presentment for any offense against the laws of the United States, and by existing laws, bail or recognizance may be taken for the appearance for trial of such person, it shall be the duty of said Judge at once to discharge such person upon bail or recognizance, for trial as aforesaid. And in case the said Secretaries of State and War shall for any reason refuse or omit to furnish the said list of persons held as prisoners aforesaid at the time of the passage of this Act, within twenty days thereafter, and of such persons as hereafter may be arrested, within twenty days from the time of the arrest, any citizen may, after a Grand Jury shall have terminated its session without finding an indictment or presentment, as provided in the second section of this Act, by a petition alleging the facts aforesaid touching any of the persons so as aforesaid imprisoned, supported by the oath of such petitioner or any other credible person, obtain and be entitled to have the said Judge's order to discharge such prisoner on the same terms and conditions prescribed in the second section of this Act; *provided*, however, that the said Judge shall be satisfied such allegations are true.

www.ingramcontent.com/pod-product-compliance
Lightning Source LLC
Chambersburg PA
CBHW032135080426
42733CB00008B/1076